Popular Rock Superstars of Yesterday and Today
POP ROCK

AC/DC	**Elton John**
Aerosmith	**The Grateful Dead**
The Allman Brothers Band	**Led Zeppelin**
The Beatles	**Lynyrd Skynyrd**
Billy Joel	**Pink Floyd**
Bob Marley and the Wailers	**Queen**
Bruce Springsteen	**The Rolling Stones**
The Doors	**U2**
	The Who

AC/DC

Ethan Schlesinger

Mason Crest Publishers

AC/DC

FRONTIS Together, Malcolm Young, Phil Rudd, Angus Young, Cliff Williams, and Brian Johnson—AC/DC—make up one of the most successful bands in rock history.

Produced by 21st Century Publishing and Communications, Inc.

Editorial by Harding House Publishing Services, Inc.

MASON CREST PUBLISHERS INC.
370 Reed Road
Broomall, Pennsylvania 19008
(866) MCP-BOOK (toll free)
www.masoncrest.com

Printed in the United States.

First Printing

9 8 7 6 5 4 3 2 1

Library of Congress Cataloging-in-Publication Data

Schlesinger, Ethan.
   AC/DC / Ethan Schlesinger.
     p. cm. — (Popular rock superstars of yesterday and today)
   Includes index.
   Hardback edition: ISBN-13: 978-1-4222-0183-1
   Paperback edition: ISBN-13: 978-1-4222-0308-8
 1. AC/DC (Musical group)—Juvenile literature. 2. Rock musicians—Australia—
Juvenile literature. I. Title.
ML3930.A16S35 2008
782.42166092'2—dc22
[B]   2007019392

Publisher's notes:
- All quotations in this book come from original sources, and contain the spelling and grammatical inconsistencies of the original text.

- The Web sites mentioned in this book were active at the time of publication. The publisher is not responsible for Web sites that have changed their addresses or discontinued operation since the date of publication. The publisher will review and update the Web site addresses each time the book is reprinted.

CONTENTS

ROCK 'N' ROLL TIMELINE

1951
"Rocket 88," considered by many to be the first rock single, is released by Ike Turner.

1969
The Woodstock Music and Arts Festival attracts a huge crowd to rural upstate New York.

1952
DJ Alan Freed coins and popularizes the term "Rock and Roll," proclaimes himself the "Father of Rock and Roll," and declares, "Rock and Roll is a river of music that has absorbed many streams: rhythm and blues, jazz, rag time, cowboy songs, country songs, folk songs. All have contributed to the Big Beat."

1969
Tommy, the first rock opera, is released by British rock band The Who.

1970
The Beatles break up.

1955
"Rock Around the Clock" by Bill Haley & His Comets is released; it tops the U.S. charts and becomes wildly popular in Britain, Australia, and Germany.

1967
The Monterey Pop Festival in California kicks off open air rock concerts.

1971
Jim Morrison, lead singer of The Doors, dies in Paris.

1965
The psychedelic rock band, the Grateful Dead, is formed in San Francisco.

1971
Duane Allman, lead guitarist of the Allman Brothers Band, dies.

1950s   1960s   1970s

1957
Bill Haley tours Europe.

1969
A rock concert held at Altamont Speedway in California is marred by violence.

1974
Sheer Heart Attack by the British rock band Queen becomes an international success.

1957
Jerry Lee Lewis and Buddy Holly become the first rock musicians to tour Australia.

1969
The Rolling Stones tour America as "The Greatest Rock and Roll Band in the World."

1954
Elvis Presley releases the extremely popular single "That's All Right (Mama)."

1961
The first Grammy for Best Rock 'n' Roll Recording is awarded to Chubby Checker for *Let's Twist Again*.

1974
"Sweet Home Alabama" by Southern rock band Lynyrd Skynyrd is released and becomes an American anthem.

1964
The Beatles make their first visit to America, setting off the British Invasion.

1973
Rolling Stone magazine names Annie Leibovitz chief photographer and "rock 'n' roll photographer;" she follows and photographs rockers Mick Jagger, John Lennon, and others.

1987
Billy Joel becomes the first American rock star to perform in the Soviet Union since the construction of the Berlin Wall.

2005
Led Zeppelin is ranked #1 on VH1's list of the 100 Greatest Artists of Hard Rock.

2005
Many rock groups participate in Live 8, a series of concerts to raise awareness of extreme poverty in Africa.

1985
Rock stars perform at Live Aid, a benefit concert to raise money to fight Ethiopian famine.

2003
Led Zeppelin's "Stairway to Heaven" is inducted into the Grammy Hall of Fame.

1980
John Lennon of the Beatles is murdered in New York City.

2000s
Aerosmith's album sales reach 140 million worldwide and the group becomes the bestselling American hard rock band of all time.

2007
Billy Joel become the first person to sing the National Anthem before two Super Bowls.

1975
Tommy, the movie, is released.

1975
Time magazine features Bruce Springsteen on its cover as "Rock's New Sensation."

1995
The Rock and Roll Hall of Fame and Museum opens in Cleveland, Ohio.

1970s   1980s   1990s   2000s

1979
Pink Floyd's *The Wall* is released.

1991
Freddie Mercury, lead vocalist of the British rock group Queen, dies of AIDS.

2004
Elton John receives a Kennedy Center Honor.

1979
The first Grammy for Best Rock Vocal Performance by a Duo or Group is awarded to The Eagles.

2004
Rolling Stone Magazine ranks The Beatles #1 of the 100 Greatest Artists of All Time, and Bob Dylan #2.

1986
The Rolling Stones receive a Grammy Lifetime Achievement Award.

1981
MTV goes on the air.

2006
U2 wins five more Grammys, for a total of 22—the most of any rock artist or group.

1981
For Those About to Rock We Salute You by Australian rock band AC/DC becomes the first hard rock album to reach #1 in the U.S.

1986
The first Rock and Roll Hall of Fame induction ceremony is held; Chuck Berry, Little Richard, Ray Charles, Elvis Presley, and James Brown, are among the first inductees.

2006
Bob Dylan, at age 65, releases *Modern Times* which immediately rises to #1 in the U.S.

In 2003, AC/DC achieved a sure sign of the group's importance in rock history—induction into the Rock and Roll Hall of Fame. After the speeches, the fun began. Aerosmith's Steven Tyler (back right) joins Brian (back left) and Angus Young (front, in his characteristic short pants) for a rousing jam session.

1

Highway to the Hall

The audience was filled with some of the biggest names in the music industry. They were all there to watch as the Clash, Elvis Costello and the Attractions, and the Police, among others, were **inducted** into the Rock and Roll Hall of Fame. One of the "others" was AC/DC, perhaps the best known rock group to come out of Australia.

The Hall

Entry into a hall of fame is a crowning achievement in many fields. Like those who become members of the Baseball Hall of Fame, the Football Hall of Fame, and similar halls, membership in the Rock and Roll Hall of Fame has to be earned. Inductees must meet the tough standards the nominating committee of the Rock and Roll Hall of Fame requires just to put a musician's name on the ballot. According to Rock and Roll Hall of Fame rules, twenty-five years must have passed since a potential nominee's first recording. Those considered for nomination must have made a significant contribution to the development of rock music. Those who meet the **criteria** are placed on the ballot, which is sent to music experts all over the world. To be inducted, the nominee must have the most votes, and be selected on more than 50 percent of the ballots.

Even the building housing the hall is special. A large, eight-story glass pyramid rises from the shore of Lake Erie. The pyramid leads to a futuristic building constructed of simple geometric shapes. According to the designer, I. M. Pei, who also designed such buildings as the Javits Convention Center in New York City and the Pyramide du Louvre in Paris, he wanted the structure to "express the **dynamic** music it celebrates." And in 2003, the hall welcomed a very dynamic group—AC/DC.

Presenting AC/DC

The March 10, 2003, induction ceremonies took place at the famous Waldorf-Astoria Hotel in New York City. The glamorous ballroom hosted many for whom tuxedoes and gowns were out-of-the-ordinary garb. Still, all were there for one purpose—to pay **homage** to some of the most significant players in rock history.

Each inductee is presented to the hall by another in the music industry. Aerosmith frontman Steven Tyler presented AC/DC. In his presentation speech, he singled out the group's use of the power chord, calling it, "the thunder from down under that gives you the . . . powerful surge that can flow through your body."

Then it was time for AC/DC. Band members thanked the millions of fans who had supported them during the group's thirty-year history. In his acceptance speech, Brian Johnson quoted from the group's "Let There Be Rock":

"In the beginning, back in 1955, man didn't know about the rock 'n roll show and all that jive. The white man had the schmaltz, the black man had the blues, but no one knew what they was gonna do but Tchaikovsky had the news, he said: let there be rock."

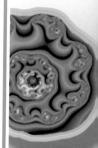

The fancy ballroom of the Waldorf-Astoria Hotel hosted the Rock and Roll Hall of Fame induction ceremonies. Steven Tyler presented the group for its induction, referring to the group's sound as "the thunder from down under." That thunder has rumbled all over the world for more than thirty years, and shows no sign of disappearing.

Thunder in the Hall

The presentation and acceptance speeches over, it was time to rock. The band played its famous "Highway to Hell" and "Back in Black." Reporting for MTV.com, Kurt Loder described the band's performance of "Highway to Hell":

❝And then, all of a sudden, like a truck bomb in a brickyard, AC/DC happened. There they were, with guitarist Angus Young duck-walking across the stage, ripping out the chords to 'Highway to Hell,' while Brian Johnson launched his power-drill shriek up toward the (relatively) cheap seats [seats at the ceremony can cost more than $1,500—each].❞

A reporter for CNN called the chorus of the latter song "loud enough to peel paint"!

Steven Tyler joined the group for "You Shook Me All Night Long," a performance that shook all of those in the audience, and during which, writes Loder, "you could almost hear brains hemorrhaging around the room." It was an awards ceremony unlike most. According to Loder:

❝There's a tiresome sense of decorum that's built into most award shows, and it tends to mute all things rude and unruly. AC/DC are apparently unaware of this. They may be unaware of anything apart from what . . . Steven Tyler . . . called 'the majesty of the power chord.'❞

It was a night like many in the crowd had never before experienced, and probably wouldn't ever again.

Coming to the Aid of a City

Toronto, Ontario, Canada faced a difficult time in 2003. Tourism plays a large role in Toronto's economy, but in early 2003, the tourism industry took a big hit when an outbreak of severe acute respiratory syndrome—SARS, a severe form of pneumonia—occurred in Toronto and other parts of Canada.

To help the city get back on its feet, the Rolling Stones decided to headline a benefit concert, and AC/DC quickly agreed to participate, despite the fact that the World Health Organization (WHO) still had Toronto under a SARS warning. Canadian brewery Molson Canadian agreed to sponsor the concert.

Whether it's called Toronto Rocks, Molson Canada Rocks for Toronto, or the Rolling Stones SARS Benefit Concert, it was a huge

A record-setting crowd of almost half a million people attended Toronto Rocks, Molson Canada Rocks, or whatever you wanted to call it. Organized by the Rolling Stones, the concert was to aid the city of Toronto, which took an economic hit when cases of SARS were found there. AC/DC was one of the groups coming to the city's aid.

success. Almost a half a million people attended the July 30, 2003, concert, making it the largest ticketed event to ever be held in the country.

Concerts earlier in the afternoon featured less well-known groups. The big guns hit the concert stage in the early evening. And did the crowds ever love AC/DC! The group was as popular as it had ever been. Not bad for a group from a country perhaps best know for koalas and kangaroos.

The Young brothers loved music, and when they moved with their family from Scotland to Australia, they found others there who shared their devotion. Before long, AC/DC was a group. Bon Scott (another Scotland native), Phil Rudd, Angus Young, Cliff Williams, and Malcolm Young pose for this photo from the early 1970s.

2

The Current Sparks

When the Young family left its native Glasgow, Scotland, in 1963, no one could have known that two of the brothers—Angus and Malcolm— would become responsible for the creation of one of the biggest bands in rock history. Nor could anyone have expected that one of the brothers would find fame in a schoolboy uniform.

Angus, the youngest of the Young brothers, was born in 1955; Malcolm was born in 1953. Both of them joined older brother George, who quickly found a band to join when the family moved to Sydney, Australia. Angus and Malcolm looked on as George found international success in the group Easybeats, an Australian **beat band**. The Easybeats were one of the country's most popular bands of the sixties, and George's success inspired Malcolm to look for a band of his own.

20222769

Malcolm found such a group when he hooked up to play guitar with the Velvet Underground, based in New South Wales, Australia. When that group broke up, Malcolm looked closer to home for a new group. He found it in his little brother, Angus, who was considered the best musician of the Young brothers. Angus also had a lot of energy, and Malcolm, showing early business **savvy**, sensed that a rock group built around his little brother would probably be successful.

Becoming AC/DC

In November 1973, Malcolm talked to Angus about forming a group. Angus was playing in a group called Kantuckee, which re-formed as Tantrum. The group had limited success, but Malcolm was very convincing, and Angus agreed. Joining Malcolm and Angus were Larry Van Kriedt on bass, Colin Burgess on drums, and on vocals, Dave Evans. AC/DC was born.

AC/DC? Group names were unusual in the early seventies (and before and after), but the name AC/DC seemed to be a bit odder than most. According to Malcolm and Angus, they wanted a name that said something about the group's energy level; after all, that was one of the reasons Malcolm had wanted to start a group with Angus. According to stories the brothers have told over the years, the name came when they saw AC/DC on the back of their sister Margaret's sewing machine. To the brothers, it implied electricity and just a bit of danger. According to the brothers, it was not until later that they were told that the acronym also stood for bisexuality.

Over the years other explanations have been given for the band's name, usually ones that imply the group members are Satanists. These alternative names include Anti-Christ/Devil's Child, After Christ/Devil Comes, and Anti-Christ/Demon Child. Despite these and other allegations, the band has always denied that the name stands for anything other than electricity.

Setting a Lineup

A month later, AC/DC had its first gig, a New Year's Eve performance at Chequers, a popular club in Sydney. Before long, the group had a record contract and released its first single, "Can I Sit Next to You." Unfortunately, the group began to suffer a fate experienced by many rock bands during their early days—a revolving door of membership.

Colin Burgess, AC/DC's drummer, had been a member of the group the Master's Apprentices before he joined the Young brothers. Despite his experience, Colin just wasn't a good fit with AC/DC, so he was fired. The group had problems with bass players as well, and audiences could never be sure who would be playing drums and bass when AC/DC performed.

AC/DC had a bigger problem when it came to its lead vocalist. The Youngs wanted the group to play hard-driving rock 'n' roll. Dave Evans appeared to have different ideas for the direction the group should go in.

During the early 1970s, glam rock (sometimes called glitter rock) was big in England. T. Rex's Marc Bolan is often credited as its creator.

For a group to succeed, it helps if all of the members are in agreement about what kind of music to play—and how to perform it. That wasn't always the case with AC/DC. The group's first lead singer, Dave Evans (far left), wasn't a good fit with the rest of the group members and their musical goals.

Other glam rockers included the early Elton John, David Bowie in his Ziggy Stardust phase, Gary Glitter, and Alice Cooper. Musicians often dressed in ways that made it unclear whether they were male or female. Showmanship was the rule. The cult classic film *The Rocky Horror Picture Show* gives you a good idea of what glam rock was all about.

The Youngs thought Dave was too much of a glam rocker; specifically, too much like Gary Glitter. He also had problems with

Searching for Dave's replacement, the band didn't have to look too far. George Young, the older brother of Angus and Malcolm, had just the guy: his friend Bon Scott. The guys listened to Bon, and they agreed—Bon would be the perfect addition to their group. With him on board, AC/DC was on its way to success.

the group's then-manager, Dennis Laughlin, who the Youngs sometimes asked to fill in for Dave. Eventually, Dave was fired. For a while, Dennis fronted the group. George's friend Ronald "Bon" Scott, another Scottish immigrant who also sometimes served as the band's driver, told him that he'd like a chance to sing. He had experience, the guys liked what they heard at his audition, and Bon became a member of AC/DC in September 1974. Shortly after Bon was in place, Mark Evans and Phil Rudd were hired to play bass and drums, respectively. The lineup was set.

What *Is* That Guy Wearing?

"So I stood there and this band comes on and there's this little guy, about that big, with a school uniform and a bag on his back going crazy and I laughed, and I must have laughed for half an hour."

That's how Bon described his first look at Angus in action. Almost from the beginning, Angus had taken to wearing costumes during AC/DC performances. After trying out other costumes, including Spiderman, a gorilla, and "Super-Ang," a take-off on Superman, Angus settled on a school uniform—complete with book bag. The uniform became almost as much a symbol of the group as did its sound!

During the 1970s, there were few groups hotter than AC/DC. The guys had quickly earned a reputation as a hard-working and hard-rocking band. But they had also earned a reputation as one of the hardest-partying groups in rock. Considering the reputations of some of the other bands of the era, that took a lot of work, too.

3

"The Thunder from Down Under"

With a set lineup of experienced musicians, a lead singer who shared the same musical goals as the rest of the guys, and a wired guitarist in a school uniform, AC/DC was ready to take on the music world. The question would be whether the music world was ready for AC/DC.

The Beginning of Success

Beginning in 1974, AC/DC made regular appearances on *Countdown*, an Australian music television program. Like many groups in Australia and all over the world, appearances on television shows of this type could make a group. And that it did for AC/DC.

With a fan base already established thanks to *Countdown*, in November 1974, AC/DC recorded its first album, *High Voltage*, which was available only in Australia and New Zealand. By December 1975, the album was certified triple gold. Bon wrote the lyrics for the album's songs, and the multitalented Malcolm and Angus wrote the music. The single "It's a Long Way to the Top (If You Wanna Rock 'n' Roll)" was then included on the group's follow-up album, *T.N.T.* Like *High Voltage*, both the single and the album were released only in Australia and New Zealand. "It's a Long Way to the Top" quickly became a fan favorite and a staple at AC/DC performances.

By early 1976, based largely on its appearances on *Countdown*, the group became one of the most successful rock bands in Australia. But to reach its potential, the guys knew they had to expand their musical reach beyond Australia and New Zealand. They had to go international.

Reaching the World

One of the first steps AC/DC took to gain an international following was to establish a base of operations in the United Kingdom. The group signed a recording contract with Atlantic Records, one of the biggest labels of the day. The label took the group's first two albums, combined tracks from each (but mostly from *T.N.T.*), and issued the resulting album in 1976, also called *High Voltage*, which was sold internationally. And it was a megahit—far beyond what anyone could have hoped.

Atlantic Records set up club dates for the group, including shows at the important Marquee Club. The label also put the group on an almost-constant touring schedule of spots in the United Kingdom and Europe. During those early days with Atlantic, AC/DC opened for such rock powerhouses as KISS, Aerosmith, and Styx. The group got its first headliner gig when they shared top billing with Cheap Trick.

In June 1976, AC/DC embarked on its first headlining tour in the United Kingdom. The tour was called Lock Up Your Daughters in reference to a lyric from the group's song "T.N.T.":

> " I'm a wanted man
> Public enemy number one
> Understand
> So lock up your daughter
> Lock up your wife
> Lock up your back door
> And run for your life. "

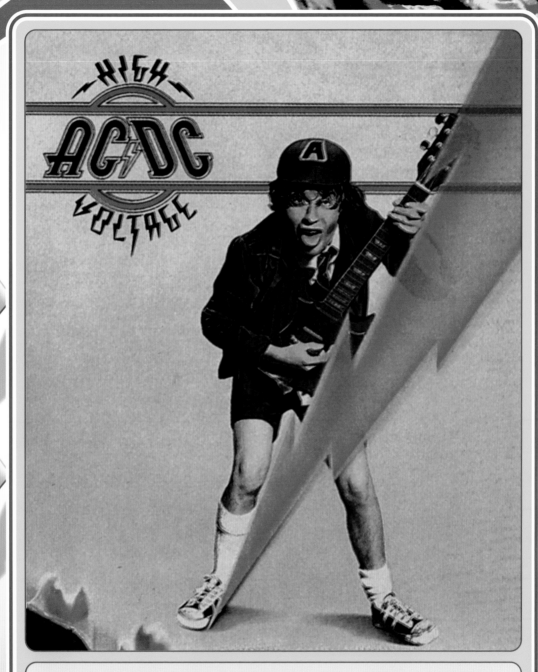

Who would have believed that one of the biggest names in rock would have a guitarist in a school uniform—complete with cap, book bag, and, oh yeah, short pants? Probably no one, but it worked for AC/DC. Angus is featured on the cover of the group's first international hit album, *High Velocity*.

When Bon Scott joined the group, things just seemed to click for the Australian band. It quickly found its footing—and a place for itself on the rock music scene. Bon also added to the band's reputation as a hard-living group. After all, he was the one with a criminal record.

Though it was just a song lyric, many thought it wasn't necessarily a bad suggestion to parents when the group came to town. AC/DC had quickly earned a reputation as a hard-working—and hard-partying—group. According to VH1.com, Bon played a large role in developing that reputation:

> **"He helped cement the group's image as brutes—he had several convictions on minor criminal offenses and was rejected by the Australian Army for being 'socially maladjusted.' And AC/DC *was* socially maladjusted. Throughout their career, they favored crude double entendres and violent imagery, all spiked with a mischievous sense of fun."**

And really, what *were* parents to think about a grown man romping onstage in a schoolboy uniform—complete with short pants? And when Angus made a habit of mooning the audience during performances, parents can probably be forgiven for being concerned about the group and its effects on their children.

Punk Rock/Hard Rock: What Kind of Rock?

The international version of *High Voltage* caught the attention of the entire music world. Perhaps some of the most enthusiastic fans were punk rockers in the United Kingdom; even the British press associated AC/DC with punk because of the group's popularity with the style's fans. Punk rock was a movement that developed in the United Kingdom, the United States, and Australia during the mid- and late 1970s. To describe the style in its most basic terms, it was everything the mainstream rock music was not. Its lyrics were **anti-authoritarian**, songs were short and fast, and instrumentation was bare-bone; some songs took advantage of only two or three chords.

So what did this have to do with AC/DC? Not much really, though punk fans did provide the group with a strong and dependable fan base. And the group's lyrics did grate on the sensibilities of the older, establishment crowd. Still the members of AC/DC refused to be categorized as punk rockers; they were a hard rock band that played music its fans liked. According to the Rock and Roll Hall of Fame:

> **AC/DC's songs had a straightforward appeal that made them more of a hard rock than a heavy metal band. . . . Their unwavering devotion to no-frills rock with plenty of bawdy wit has made for a consistency that's won them the loyalty of millions of fans.**

The hard-rock style of music can trace its roots to the 1960s and garage bands and **psychedelic** rock. The music has a strong blues influence, and distorted electric guitars, bass, and drums—but guitars rule. The guitarist is the dominant force in most hard rock groups. And this can certainly be seen in AC/DC. The group is perhaps best known for its use of the power chord, a perfect fifth or fourth played on an electric guitar with distortion, which is a characteristic technique of hard rock. The chord consists of only two notes; it does not have the note that designates whether the chord is major or minor. The term "power chord" also refers to the sonic effect caused by the combination of two notes separated by the interval of a perfect fifth (or a perfect fourth) when distorted, usually through an amplifier or an electronic processor. Even though AC/DC was not the first to use the technique, few others have used it as effectively, and AC/DC was sometimes criticized for using it as often as they did. Angus commented on that criticism:

> **It's just rock and roll. A lot of times we get criticized for it. A lot of music papers come out with: 'When are they going to stop playing these three chords?' If you believe you shouldn't play just three chords it's pretty silly on their part. To us, the simpler a song is, the better, 'cause it's more in line with what the person on the street is.**

Angus knew what he was talking about. After all, the use of power chords earned the group the nickname "the thunder from down under."

Winning Over America

In 1977, AC/DC recorded *Let There Be Rock*. For the first time, an AC/DC album was released simultaneously all over the world. The closest the group had previously come to doing so was 1976's *Dirty*

At 5' 2" tall, Angus Young didn't necessarily look the part of a rock powerhouse—especially when you factor in his schoolboy costume. Nonetheless, Angus was one of the keys to the band's unique sound, and one of the band's most energetic and most appreciated entertainers—at least among its fans. Parents weren't quite sure what to make of the guy.

Deeds Done Dirt Cheap. That album was released in Australia and internationally the same year, but the track list was different on the versions. (*Dirty Deeds* wouldn't be released in the United States until 1981.) The band also released something else in 1977. Well, some*one* else: Mark Evans.

Why Mark left the group is another of rock history's mysteries. Some say he was tired of the group's heavy tour schedule. Others claim there were serious personal conflicts between Malcolm and Mark. Malcolm and Angus never commented on why Mark left the group. In his book *Highway to Hell: The Life and Times of AC/DC Legend Bon Scott*, author Clinton Walker quotes the band's booking manager at the time, Richard Griffiths: "You knew Mark wasn't going to last, he was just too much of a nice guy." Cliff Williams was named to replace Mark.

The United States beckoned AC/DC in 1977. Radio station WTAC AM 600, located in Flint, Michigan, booked the group for a concert at the city's Capitol Theater. WTAC was a popular top-40 station in the 1960s and 1970s. During rock's early days, it was an important station, owned at one time by the Chess brothers, who also owned Chess Records, a record label responsible for recording and releasing some of the blues' and early rock's biggest hits. (Today, WTAC is an FM station; AM 600 now broadcasts Christian music.)

The concert opened with a performance by MC5, who reunited and agreed to perform for this special occasion. But the crowd was there to see AC/DC, and it erupted when the group took the stage. Though some in the crowd weren't sure how to take the group, especially Angus's antics, most were enthusiastic fans. The band pounded out its rhythms and was rewarded with cheers and ovations.

Highway to Hell

The band was back in the studio in 1978, the first time with Cliff on bass. The result, *Powerage*, wasn't an overwhelming success, though it did sell a million copies in the United States. A year later, AC/DC released one of its biggest successes, *Highway to Hell*. Until then, George Young and Harry Vanda had produced the group's albums. In 1979, it was decided that the next album would be recorded in England, rather than in Australia. George also talked to his brothers about a new producer for the album. Malcolm and Angus agreed,

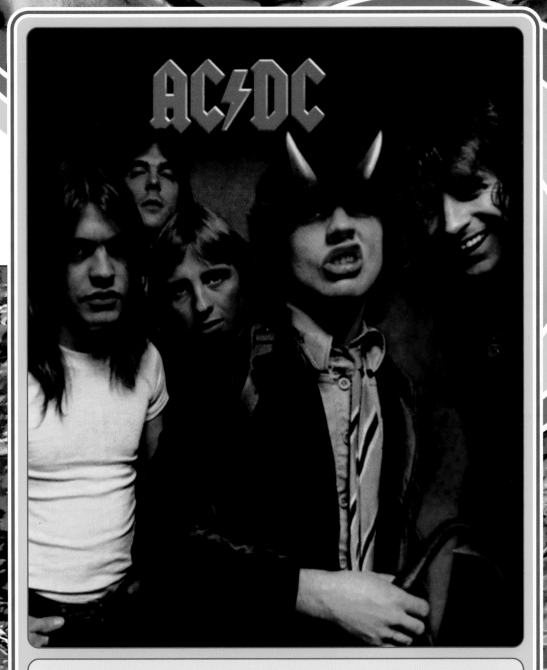

If the band had any intention of becoming a parent favorite, its 1979 *Highway to Hell* may have nipped it in the bud. The music wasn't the only thing that caused problems for some people. Many found Angus's horns on the album cover objectionable. Some believed the horns meant he was a Satanist.

and Eddie Kramer was hired to produce the album. During preproduction work in Australia, differences arose between Kramer and the band, however, and he was fired. John "Mutt" Lange came on board to produce what became *Highway to Hell*. Though this was early in Lange's career, he would go on to produce more albums for AC/DC as well as albums for musicians as **diverse** as Def Leppard and Shania Twain (whom he married). Tracks for the album were recorded in Miami, Florida, as well as in London.

When *Highway to Hell* was released, the group found itself the focus of new adoring fans. The group's popularity grew as the album

Along with hit albums and singles, AC/DC also experienced the tragedy that seems to follow some of rock's biggest bands. In 1980, Bon Scott died from acute alcohol poisoning. But that's just what the official report says. Some fans believe there was another, more sinister, cause of the rock star's death.

climbed the charts, reaching #17 in the United States, its first album to crack the *Billboard* top-100 album charts. With the album's release and the supporting tour, AC/DC was on top of the hard-rock world.

The group was on top of the controversy charts as well. The album cover featured a picture of Angus sprouting horns. During the album tour, Angus often wore a jacket that had a pair of horns on it. To some, this proved that the group—or at least Angus—had satanic leanings. It also renewed the question of what AC/DC *really* stood for. But controversy aside, there was no arguing with success. AC/DC was on top and planned to stay that way.

Farewell Bonny Scot

It's funny how things work. Just when you think you've got it made, the world sometimes gets kicked out from under you. In a way, that's what happened to AC/DC on February 19, 1980.

Ronald Belford "Bon" Scott loved everything about being part of a successful rock band. In fact, Bon probably loved it too much. Bon worked hard, but he partied hard too. According to official reports, Bon was out partying one night in February. He passed out in his friend Alistair Kinnear's car. Kinnear left him there. The next morning, Kinnear went to check on Bon, who was unconscious. He was rushed to the hospital, where he pronounced DOA—dead on arrival. The official autopsy listed the cause of death as acute alcohol poisoning and his death a "misadventure."

When someone famous dies, it's not uncommon for rumors of a conspiracy or talk of "the *real* cause of death" to begin to circulate. This was certainly true in the case of Bon's death, and these rumors have continued to the present day. Some people believe Bon died from a heroin overdose. That Bon **asphyxiated** on his own vomit is another popular theory. Some even believe it was murder, or perhaps suicide from breathing the fumes from the car's exhaust. Even the existence of Alistair Kinnear has been called into question by those who prefer a more mysterious cause of the rock star's death.

No matter what the cause of Bon's death, it left his fans and the surviving members of AC/DC in a state of shock and grief. Angus, Malcolm, Cliff, and Phil were also faced with a big question: What should they do next?

It's not unusual for a group to have a change in membership, and AC/DC had certainly found that to be the case. But when a group's lead vocalist and a cowriter of its biggest hits dies, it's only natural for everyone to wonder if the band can go on. AC/DC, its fans, and its critics wondered—but not for long.

Recharged

Highway to Hell earned AC/DC the fame and respect that all rock groups strive for. People all over the world knew who AC/DC was, and it wasn't just the members' onstage antics that drew fans to concerts and into record stores to buy its albums. But now, without Bon, fans and critics wondered if the band could go on.

It wasn't just the fans and critics who wondered about AC/DC's future; so did the surviving band members. Though Angus was the one who seemed to grab the fans' attention during performances, Bon was the lead singer, the voice of the group. After considering the idea of ending the group, Angus, Malcolm, Cliff, and Phil decided the group had to go on. Malcolm and Angus began work on material for a new album. In an interview with *Rolling Stone* magazine, Malcolm said, "I just rang up Angus and said, 'Do you wanna come back and rehearse?'" AC/DC would survive. But they needed a new lead singer.

Finding a New Vocalist

It was going to take someone extremely talented to be AC/DC's new frontman. Angus, Malcolm, Cliff, and Phil knew they'd never be able to *replace* Bon, but they could find the best person out there to assume the lead vocalist duties. One of the first singers considered was Terry Slesser, who had performed with Back Street Crawler. Though flattered, Terry wanted to work on a solo career rather than sing in another group. Moxy vocalist Buzz Shearman was also asked to join AC/DC, but he was suffering from problems with his voice, so he couldn't sign on with the band.

Brian Johnson, who had been the lead vocalist for Geordie, a glam rock band that had split up in the late seventies, was next asked to audition. Malcolm, Angus, Cliff, and Phil were impressed with what they heard, and a few days later, they asked Brian to join the group. Though he had just re-formed Geordie and signed a record deal, he agreed. AC/DC was again complete.

Bon had been familiar with the singer who was now going to sing lead for AC/DC. In a 2003 interview, Angus told the *Guardian*, a British newspaper, a story Bon had once told him about seeing Brian perform in person:

> **"I remember Bon playing me 'Little Richard' and then telling me the story of when he saw Brian singing. And he says about that night, 'there's this guy up there screaming at the top of his lungs and then the next thing you know, he hits the deck. He's on the floor, rolling around and screaming. I thought it was great, and then to top it off—you couldn't get a better encore—they came in and wheeled the guy off!'"**

Bon might have been impressed by the theatrics, but it wasn't the music that led to Brian's inspired movements that night; it was something much more basic—pain. Later that night, Brian underwent surgery for appendicitis.

AC/DC Is Back

Malcolm, Angus, Cliff, and Phil were comfortable with Brian on lead vocals, but the question remained: How would AC/DC fans accept

After auditioning several singers, Brian Johnson (shown here in the center, kicking a hat) was selected to join AC/DC as its lead vocalist. Even Bon had been a fan of the former Geordie frontman. When Brian took over the vocalist responsibilities, the group didn't skip a beat on its climb up the ladder of success.

the new lead vocalist? That question would be answered with *Back in Black*, the group's next album. Work had begun on the album while Bon was still alive, and now, with Brian on board, Malcolm and Angus finished writing the songs for the album.

When *Back in Black* was released in late 1980, it hit the charts quickly and hard. Within a year, the album was certified **platinum**. As of the end of 2006, the album had sold more than 21 million copies in the United States alone! It spent an amazing 131 weeks in the top-10 on the *Billboard* album charts in the United States.

The album spawned three hit singles as well: "Hells Bells," "You Shook Me All Night Long," and "Back in Black." "Hells Bells" opens with the ringing of a two-ton bell. Why? According to Angus:

> **"I like the bell 'cause it makes a brilliant sound and it was fitting for the time we went through after Bon's death and *Back in Black* and so on. It was part of the situation at the time."**

The bells weren't the group's only tribute to its late lead singer. The all-black cover and even the title were tributes to Bon.

Fans weren't the only ones impressed with *Back in Black*. Critics were enthusiastic about the album as well. According to the Rock and Roll Hall of Fame, the album shot the group into the realm of legend:

> **"The music rocked with a determined authority that catapulted AC/DC into a class with Led Zeppelin, Deep Purple, and the Rolling Stones. Because they were younger than those bands, AC/DC bonded with a youthful audience that kept them on top throughout the 1980s. *Back in Black* was an instant classic."**

Even Bigger

In an industry in which a group is only as big as its latest hit, Malcolm, Angus, Brian, Cliff, and Phil knew their next album had to be bigger than *Back in Black*. And they succeeded with 1981's *For Those About to Rock (We Salute You)*. Fans and critics alike loved the album. It became the group's first album to top the album charts in the United States. More than a million copies sold the first week it was released.

This album also spun off successful singles, including "Let's Get It Up" and "For Those About to Rock (We Salute You)." The title track was recorded live and opens with the firing of cannons. Malcolm wasn't sure the cannons were an effective or good idea:

> **"Those cannons, I'm not sure about. If it was a real cannon out there and we could blow everyone's brains out, then that would be GREAT."**

Perhaps musicians aren't always the best judges of what are good things.

If Brian thought he'd be carrying the band once he joined, it is probably a safe assumption that carrying guitar-playing Angus onto the stage was not exactly what he had in mind. Nevertheless, that's exactly what Brian did during a performance. AC/DC proved it had lost none of its showmanship.

When it comes to an AC/DC concert, bigger has always been better. And there was no question that a cannon on stage certainly made a *big* impression—whether or not Angus was playing on top of it. Malcolm wasn't sure it was a good thing, though he did acknowledge that really firing one would have had quite an impact.

Banking on the group's latest—and biggest—success, AC/DC was asked to headline the Monsters of Rock in Donington, England, in 1981. The concert was held at the Castle Donington Race Track, a facility that could hold 100,000 fans. Joining the group on the bill were Whitesnake, Blue Öyster Cult, Slade, Blackfoot, and More. The decision to put AC/DC on the bill proved to be a wise one; the crowds went crazy when the band launched into its hits. The group would headline again in 1984 (other performers included Van Halen and Ozzy Osbourne) and 1991 (along with, among others, the Black Crowes and Metallica).

Trouble in Paradise

As great as 1981 had been, AC/DC should probably have expected that they could not escape pitfalls that had plagued other groups throughout the history of music. Arguments and addiction are at the top of this list.

Bon's death affected Phil perhaps more than other members of the group. Adding to his problems coping with Bon's death, Phil had a growing problem with alcohol. After a while, Phil's long-time friendship with Malcolm began to suffer. It certainly didn't help that Malcolm was also dealing with his own addiction to alcohol. Arguments between Phil and Malcolm grew increasingly frequent and more heated, until one day, the pair erupted into a physical fight. Phil was fired immediately.

The group was in the middle of recording its next album when Phil was fired. Phil had laid down most of the drum tracks for the album before leaving the group. A session musician came in to finish the tracks, but none of those tracks were used. The group held an audition, and Simon Wright was hired to replace Phil on drums.

But Phil wasn't the only problem for the group. Mutt Lange had produced two of AC/DC's most successful albums. For the next one, *Flick of the Switch*, the guys decided to change producers once again. This time, they would self-produce the album, which was released in 1984. Looking back, that might not have been the wisest of decisions. Critics didn't care for the album, writing that there was nothing about it to make it stand out from the group's other albums. Readers of the rock magazine *Kerrang!* voted the group the eighth biggest disappointment of 1984. The group's next album, *Fly on the Wall*, produced by Angus and Malcolm, was also not well received by critics and fans. It was beginning to look as though the group's time as a hit-maker was over.

The Climb Back

In 1985, everyone was reminded that AC/DC's success was truly international when they headlined Rock in Rio, Brazil. An estimated 500,000 fans were on hand for the classic AC/DC performance.

The group found itself back on the music charts in 1986 thanks to a fan. Well, it wasn't just any ordinary fan. Author Stephen King had been an AC/DC fan for a long time. When he needed a group to record the soundtrack to his book-turned-movie *Maximum Overdrive*, King wanted AC/DC, no one else. And they agreed. The album was called *Who Made Who*, and includes some of the group's biggest hits, along with new cuts.

Over the next couple of years, the group continued to record and tour. It seemed as though it had again found its footing. The late 1980s also found the group and its members the recipients of an important **accolade** in its home country of Australia: in February 1988, the band was inducted into the Australian Recording Industry Association Hall of Fame. Along with AC/DC, other inductees included Dame Joan Sutherland, Johnny O'Keefe, and Slim Dusty. Music producers Harry Vanda and George Young, responsible for much of the early success of AC/DC as well as high points in the careers of other musicians, were also admitted to the hall.

A Rocky End and a Promising Beginning

The 1980s had been a rocky decade for the "thunder from down under." The group had experienced some of its greatest successes and some of its less than **stellar** moments. As the decade came to a close, the group found itself back with its original producers, Vanda and Young, and with another album, *Blow Up Your Video*. Though the album, released in 1988, was a critical disappointment, it had more commercial success than the group's previous two. In the United Kingdom, the album reached #2 on the charts, the group's highest-charting album since *Back in Black*. The album sold two million copies in the United States.

Phil had been with the band for many years, but in 1981, his role in AC/DC came to a screeching halt. Alcohol addiction began to affect his relationships with the other members of the group, especially Malcolm. After one physical fight, Malcolm and the others had had enough. Phil was fired.

No.7
Vol. 3

METAL HAMMER

April 11th 1988

£ 1.40

THE INTERNATIONAL HARD ROCK & HEAVY METAL MAGAZINE

Nkr 27.50
DKr 29.00
Fmk 16.50
L 5000
SKr 24.60
ESC 520

ANTHRAX FAN MAG
15 pages!

WIN A TRIP TO NEW YORK TO SEE JUDAS PRIEST
Part Two of an Exclusive Competition

Posters:

KROKUS

ANGUS YOUNG

ANTHRAX

AC/DC
Exclusive Video Report And Discography

IRON MAIDEN
Lucky Seven: Interview & Album Review

DEF LEPPARD
Hystery In The Making

ACCEPT
— LIVE REVIEW —
Have they found the right man?

AC/DC went through more ups and downs during the 1980s than some roller coasters. Still, the band was a group to be taken seriously, as can be seen in this photo of Angus on the cover of the April 1988 issue of *Metal Hammer*, a British magazine. Despite the bad times—and those that were even worse—the band vowed to continue.

The *Blow Up Your Video* tour kicked off in Australia in February 1988. After the European leg of the tour, Malcolm suddenly announced he was leaving the tour. The reason given was that he needed to rest (after all, the group had been recording and touring almost nonstop for several years) and that he needed to care for his son who was ill. Though both reasons contained bits of the truth, Malcolm used the time away to treat his alcoholism, something that had plagued him for many years. Another Young relative, nephew Stevie, replaced Malcolm for the remaining tour dates.

Once the tour was over, the group weathered some rough spots on the way to its next album. AC/DC membership again changed. Simon left the group to work on a project with another band. He was replaced by session drummer Chris Slade. Angus and Malcolm worked on material for a new album, this time without Brian, who was taking some time away to deal with personal problems. The album that resulted, *The Razor's Edge*, released in 1990, showed no evidence of those problems. The album cracked the top-10 on the album charts and was certified multi-platinum. The tour supporting the album was one of the group's most successful. Some of the stops were recorded and released in 1992 as *Live*. Many rock historians consider that album one of the best live albums of the 1990s.

Return to Basics

By 1994, some members of the group were feeling nostalgic for the way things had once been. When the group toured New Zealand, Phil was asked to join the guys for a jam session. He agreed, and before long, Angus and the others wanted him back in the group. The guys weren't unhappy working with Chris; Angus said of him, "Slade was the best musician in AC/DC." They just wanted to return to the lineup of the early 1980s, the group's most successful period.

Phil agreed to rejoin the group, giving up his non-music life of flying helicopters, racing cars, and farming. AC/DC recorded *Ballbreaker* in 1995, and had a hit single with "Hard as a Rock." The group was back.

As the new millennium broke, AC/DC was still thrilling its fans, just as it had for almost thirty years. The group was working as hard as ever in 2000, despite what this photo might indicate. Everyone needs a little "down time," and (from bottom left to right) Malcolm, Angus, and Brian had some fun during the group's Berlin stop.

Still on the Circuit

A new decade, a new millennium, a new old AC/DC. In 2000, the guys were still rockin', just shy of thirty years as a group. Since its beginning as a band in Australia in 1973, the group had traveled the sometimes perilous route to rock success. And the path had been interrupted with detours along the way.

With Phil back on drums, the group returned to the lineup that produced *Back in Black* and *For Those About to Rock (We Salute You)*. Since Phil's departure, the group had been unable to achieve the same level of success those albums had reached. Now, with Phil back in the fold, the group looked to recapture its success.

Stiff Upper Lip

Phil's return in the 1990s brought AC/DC the commercial success the group had been lacking since Phil was fired. The band again had the sound that set them apart from other rock groups. *Stiff Upper Lip*, released in 2000, was another commercial success for AC/DC. It reached #1 on the album charts of five countries and #2 in three more. In the group's native Australia, the album reached #3. In the United States, *Stiff Upper Lip* reached #7. The title single topped the U.S. singles charts for four weeks. "Safe in New York City" and "Satellite Blues" were also successful in the United States; "Satellite Blues" reached #7 on the *Billboard* singles chart in the United States.

Though critics didn't love *Stiff Upper Lip*, they did like it more than *Ballbreaker*, but many felt it was "old," that it had been done before, and there was nothing new on the release.

The *Stiff Upper Lip* tour spread across the world, however, signifying AC/DC's international reputation as true rock legends. In the United States, stops included Michigan, Georgia, Pennsylvania, New York, Illinois, and Mississippi. The group also played gigs in Belgium, Germany, Finland, France, Scotland, England, Spain, Australia, and Japan, among other countries. Some of the sites might not have been as elaborate as they were during the group's heyday (one critic called the Mississippi site "a joke"), but millions of fans all over the world appreciated the chance to see Malcolm, Angus, Cliff, and Phil again. This time, parents who had been AC/DC fans when they were kids brought their kids to the show. A tour version of the album was released in 2001, but only in Australia.

Stiff Upper Lip was the last studio album recorded by AC/DC. The group signed a multiple album deal with Sony Records in 2002. The label **remastered** and re-released the group's catalogue in 2003, except for the two most recent albums. (*Ballbreaker* and *Stiff Upper Lip* were remastered and re-released in 2005 and 2010, respectively; a remastered *Still Upper Lip* was released in the United Kingdom in 2007.) These re-releases contain much more than just music. Fans receive a special booklet that contains photographs, memorabilia, and even notes.

In January 2006, the group announced it was working on a new album, but 2006 came and went without anything new being released. Malcolm said the delay was caused by the group's desire that it be "perfect." Brian, who was contributing to writing the album along with Malcolm and Angus, reportedly said that patient AC/DC fans might be rewarded with a double album. This is the first time since

AC/DC has shown the unique ability to hold onto its fans for decades—all the while gaining new ones. The group's original fans are now parents, who often bring their kids to AC/DC concerts. In this photo, Angus poses with a young Belgian fan, complete with the *Highway to Hell* horns.

1988 that Brian had written song lyrics for an AC/DC album. Millions of fans were eagerly waiting.

The *Family Jewels*

Though AC/DC has been slow in recording and releasing a new album, fans were treated to a special DVD release in 2005. For *Family Jewels*, the guys took bits from their television and live performance videos and combined them into the two-DVD set. The DVD begins at the beginning—the group's first performance on Australian television—and continues through the 1990s. The set also includes a 1980 performance the group gave on Spanish television just a few days before Bon's tragic death on February 19.

Getting Props

It's only a matter of time before groups that have been around as long and as successful as AC/DC are recognized for their accomplishments. Music groups and solo artists come and go. Names are added to the list of musical one-hit wonders every year. Few bands have the success and long life of AC/DC.

People love lists of the top in almost any subject. *Rolling Stone* magazine put *Back in Black* at the #73 spot on its list of the 500 Greatest Albums of All Time in 2003. But *Q* magazine, a publication in the United Kingdom that concentrates on pop/rock music, is one of the most prolific magazines that help feed pop music fans with its many lists of favorites. Over its long career, AC/DC has appeared on many *Q* magazine lists. Its first appearance was in 1996, when the group's 1981 performance at Castle Donington was named one of The Best Gigs Ever. *Let There Be Rock* made the list of the Heaviest Albums of All Time in 2001. "Whole Lotta Rosie," the live version, was #38 on the magazine's 50 Most Exciting Tunes Ever in 2002. (In the top spot was the Sex Pistols' "God Save the Queen"; at #50 was "Franklin Goes to Hollywood" by Two Tribes.) Also in 2002, AC/DC was in the #1 position on *Q*'s list of the 50 Bands to See Before You Die. (Others on the list included Tony Bennett at #2, Pink Floyd at #5, The Who at #7, Bob Dylan at #19, the Rolling Stones at #21, U2 at #42, and the Hives at #50.) The magazine surveyed its readers in 2003 to come up with the list of the 100 Greatest Albums Ever, and at #98 was AC/DC's *Back in Black*. (Nirvana's *Nevermind* topped the list, and *The Soft Bulletin*

The twenty-first century saw AC/DC getting the recognition it had long deserved. One achievement was the 2006 *Kerrang!* Legend award, which Angus holds in this photo. Angus also won another award in 2006 when *Maxim*, a men's magazine, ranked him #1 on its list of the 25 Biggest Short Dudes of All Time.

by the Flaming Lips came in at #100.) *Back in Black* returned to a *Q* list in 2006 when readers named it one of the Best Albums Ever. (Coming in at #1 on the list was Radiohead's *OK Computer*; *Yankee Hotel Foxtrot* held the #100 spot.) In 2000, VH1 put AC/DC at the #4 spot on its list of the 100 Greatest Hard Rock Artists. (Led Zeppelin topped the list. Other musicians making the list were The Who at #8, Queen at #13, Joan Jett and the Blackhearts at #66, and at #100, Quiet Riot.)

Now fans visiting Los Angeles, California, can walk all over AC/DC—well, at least their hands. In 2000, the guys added their handprints to those of other rock legends such as Aerosmith and Stevie Ray Vaughn on the Hollywood Rock Walk of Fame. Malcolm also donated a guitar to the museum's collection of rock memorabilia.

Sales and More Accolades

The measure of a group's or solo musician's success is largely based on the number of albums (or CDs) sold. In 2003, the Recording Industry Association of America (the RIAA) adjusted the group's U.S. sales numbers. Previously, the group's total sales had stood at 46.3 million, an impressive number of sales. But recalculation brought the number of units sold in the United States up to an even more impressive 63 million! This made AC/DC the fifth-best seller in the country, trailing only the Beatles, Led Zeppelin, Pink Floyd, and the Eagles. *Back in Black* was certified double diamond, indicating sales of 20 million copies. At the close of 2005, the album had sold 21 million copies in the United States and 42 million worldwide.

As of 2000, fans can walk over AC/DC. On September 15, the guys put their hands in the cement of the Hollywood Rock Walk of Fame in Los Angeles, California. They join such rock legends as Les Paul, Stevie Ray Vaughn, Carlos Santana, Aerosmith, and rock promoter Bill Graham, all of whom have been memorialized on Sunset Boulevard. Malcolm donated one of his Gretsch guitars to the museum's collection.

In March 2003, the Rock and Roll Hall of Fame opened its doors to the group. When the announcement was first made, Mark Evans' name appeared among the members who would be inducted. However, when the ceremony actually took place, his name had been "mysteriously" dropped. Inducted into the Rock and Roll Hall of Fame as members of AC/DC were current members Phil Rudd, Brian Johnson, Cliff Williams, Angus Young, and Malcolm Young, along with the late Bon Scott.

According to the Rock and Roll Hall of Fame:

"For three decades AC/DC has reigned as one of the best-loved and hardest-rocking bands in the world. Featuring guitarist Angus Young as their visual symbol and musical firebrand, they grew from humble origins in Australia to become an arena-filling phenomenon with worldwide popularity."

The Rock and Roll Hall of Fame also praised the group for its ability to refrain from gimmicks to attract fans:

> **"They did so without gimmickry, except for Angus's schoolboy uniform, which became mandatory stage attire. From the beginning they have been a straight-ahead, no-frill rock and roll band that aimed for the gut."**

Brian agreed with the Rock and Roll Hall of Fame's assessment: "We've never pulled any punches. . . . We just play music that's fun and simple—the way our audience likes it."

In May 2003, the Australasian Performing Right Association awarded Malcolm, Angus, and posthumously Bon the Ted Albert Award for Outstanding Services to Australian Music in 2003. The award is given by the organization that represents New Zealand and Australian composers, lyricists, and music publishers in recognition of lifetime achievement.

Off the Beaten Path

Sometimes awards and recognitions might not be as prestigious as induction into a hall of fame or the receipt of a lifetime achievement award. That does not mean they have no value and should not be recognized!

On March 2, 2000, the city of Leganés, Spain, honored the group by naming a street in its honor: Calle de AC/DC. Australia was not about to let its homegrown legends be without a street there. On October 1, 2004, Melbourne's Corporation Lane was officially renamed ACDC Lane. (Street names in the city cannot contain a slash mark.)

In 2006, Angus received his own special award. *Maxim*, a magazine for men, compiled its list of the 25 Biggest Short Dudes of All Time. The list was filled with politicians and world leaders (James Madison #10, Napoleon Bonaparte #3), world leader wannabes (Ross Perot #23), athletes (Doug Flutie #24, Jeff Gordon #17), fictional characters or those who played them (Yoda #6, the actors who played the Hobbits #9), and rock stars (Kurt Cobain #20, Prince #19). Topping the list as the Biggest Short Dude of All Time was none other than 5' 2" Angus Young of AC/DC!

Remembering Bon

In the years that have followed Bon's death in 1980, band members have made a point of mentioning his importance to the group.

A band *has* to be good if it can set earnings records when it isn't performing or recording. And that's exactly what AC/DC did in 2005, when the band was the second-highest-earning entertainers from Australia (the Wiggles topped the list). Though the guys are older now, they still have what it takes to grab and hold their fans.

Melbourne, Australia, paid tribute to its local heroes when it renamed Corporation Lane ACDC Lane. The decision was not without controversy; five objections were received. The city realized how diehard AC/DC fans are and it ordered additional signs to be made to replace those that would be inevitably taken as souvenirs.

Whether at the Rock and Roll Hall of Fame induction ceremony or when accepting a lifetime achievement award from the Australasian Performing Right Association, Bon's contributions to the band's success have been acknowledged.

In 2007, Bon's fans in Fremantle, Western Australia, staged a fund-raising concert to benefit the erection of a statue in his honor. When Bon's family immigrated to Australia, they made their home in Western Australia. When Bon died, Western Australia was where his family chose to have him buried. Performing at the concert were mostly Australian bands that had been influenced by Bon and AC/DC. Among them were the Angels, Rose Tattoo, the Party Boys, the Screaming Jets, Dave Warner, and the Sure Fire Midnights. Even Mark Evans, who left the group under less than friendly terms, was there to support the project. The concert was a huge success, with more than enough money contributed to fund the statue. It is expected to be in place by 2008.

Becoming a Rock Legend

It is not easy to become a rock legend. If it were, there would be more of them. To become a rock legend requires hard work, a bit of luck, and lots of talent. It also takes longevity. Malcolm Young, Angus Young, Cliff Williams, Phil Rudd had all of those; Bon had all but longevity. Few groups can claim a history that goes back more than thirty years. Even fewer can claim they are still working.

Some, like AC/DC, can make an even greater—or perhaps more unusual—claim. In 2005, the group finished second on the list of the highest-earning entertainers from Australia, and they didn't even release an album or tour in 2005! (Number one? The Wiggles.)

Other bands, such as Van Halen and Def Leppard, have looked to AC/DC for inspiration. Amazingly, AC/DC's hard-rocking guys have become role models. No wonder these musicians have become rock legends and superstars!

1963 **March 10** The Young family emigrates from Scotland to Australia.

1973 **November** AC/DC is formed.

December 31 AC/DC plays its first gig.

1974 **September** Bon Scott joins the group as lead vocalist.

AC/DC begins making regular appearances on *Countdown*, an Australian music television show.

November The group records its first album.

1975 **December** *High Voltage* is certified gold in Australia and New Zealand.

1976 The international version of *High Voltage* is released.

June The group begins its first tour as the headlining act.

1977 *Let There Be Rock* is released.

Mark Evans leaves the group; he is replaced by Cliff Williams.

The group comes to the United States for the first time.

1979 *Highway to Hell* is released, one of the group's biggest hits.

1980 **February 19** Bon Scott is found dead in a friend's car; Brian Johnson will later be named the band's new lead vocalist.

July *Back in Black* is released and is a huge success.

1981 *For Those About to Rock (We Salute You)* is released to commercial and critical success.

The band headlines the Monsters of Rock concert.

1983 Phil Rudd is fired.

1984 *Flick of the Switch* is released and proves to be a disappointment.

1985 *Fly on the Wall* is released and is another disappointment.

The band headlines Rock in Rio in Brazil.

1986 The band records the soundtrack for the Stephen King film *Maximum Overdrive*.

1988 **February** AC/DC is inducted into the Australian Recording Industry Association Hall of Fame.

1990 AC/DC finds success again with the release of *The Razor's Edge*.

1992 *Live* is released; it's considered by many to be the best live album of the 1990s.

1994 Phil is asked to rejoin the band, and he agrees.

2000 AC/DC gets a spot on the Hollywood Rock Walk of Fame.

Stiff Upper Lip is released and is a commercial success.

VH1 places AC/DC at the #4 spot on its list of the 100 Greatest Hard Rock Artists.

March 2 Leganés, Spain, names a street in AC/DC's honor.

2002 AC/DC is ranked #1 on *Q*'s list of the 50 Bands to See Before You Die.

2003 AC/DC is inducted into the Rock and Roll Hall of Fame.

The RIAA adjusts sales figures that now places AC/DC as the fifth-best seller in the country.

Back in Black is certified double diamond.

July 30 AC/DC performs at a concert to benefit the city of Toronto.

2004 **October 1** Melbourne's Corporation Lane is officially renamed ACDC Lane.

2005 *Family Jewels*, a two-disc DVD set, is released.

The group finishes second on the list of the highest-earning entertainers from Australia.

2007 A concert is held in Fremantle, Western Australia, to raise funds to erect a statue in honor of Bon Scott.

Albums

1975 *High Voltage* (Australia)
T.N.T. (Australia)

1976 *High Voltage*
Dirty Deeds Done Dirt Cheap (Australia and International)

1977 *Let There Be Rock*

1978 *If You Want Blood You've Got It*
Powerage

1979 *Highway to Hell*

1980 *Back in Black*

1981 *Dirty Deeds Done Dirt Cheap* (U.S.)
For Those About to Rock (We Salute You)

1983 *Flick of the Switch*

1984 *'74 Jailbreak*

1985 *Fly on the Wall*

1986 *Who Made Who*

1988 *Blow Up Your Video*

1990 *The Razor's Edge*

1992 *Live*

1995 *Ballbreaker*

1997 *Let There Be Rock: The Movie*
Live from the Atlantic Studios
Volts

2000 *Stiff Upper Lip*

2001 *Stiff Upper Lip Tour Edition* (Australia)

2005 *Ballbreaker* (Remaster)

2007 *Stiff Upper Lip* (Remaster, U.K.)

Number-One Singles

1993 "Big Gun"

1996 "Hard as a Rock"

2000 "Stiff Upper Lip"

Videos

2001 *No Bull*
Stiff Upper Lip

2003	*Live at Donington*
2004	*Back in Black* *Toronto Rocks*
2005	*Family Jewels* *Music in Review: Bon Scott Years*
2006	*Maximum Overdrive* *Thunder Rock*
2007	*Highway to Hell*

Select Awards/Recognitions

1988   AC/DC is inducted into the Australian Recording Industry Association Hall of Fame.

2000   AC/DC is honored on the Hollywood Rock Walk of Fame.

VH1: Ranks AC/DC #4 of the 100 Greatest Hard Rock Artists.

2001   *Q*: *Let There Be Rock* is named one of the Heaviest Albums of All Time.

2002   *Q*: AC/DC ranks #1 on list of the 50 Bands to See Before You Die.

Live version of "Whole Lotta Rosie" ranked #38 on list of 50 Most Exciting Tunes Ever.

2003   Malcolm, Angus and Bon are awarded the Ted Albert Award for Outstanding Services to Australian Music by the Australasian Performing Right Association.

AC/DC is inducted into the Rock and Roll Hall of Fame.

Rolling Stone: *Back in Black* is ranked #73 on its list of the 500 Greatest Albums of All Time.

Q: *Back in Black* ranks #98 on list of 100 Greatest Albums Ever.

2006   *Maxim*: Angus is ranked #1 on the list of the 25 Biggest Short Dudes of All Time.

Q: *Back in Black* makes the one of the Best Albums Ever list.

Books

Dome, Malcolm. *AC/DC: The Definitive History*. London: Virgin Publishing, 2002.

Eaglehart, Murray, and Arnaud Durieux. *AC/DC: Maximum Rock and Roll: The Ultimate Story of the World's Greatest Rock-and-Roll Band*. New York: HarperCollins, 2007.

Huxley, Martin. *AC/DC: The World's Heaviest Rock*. New York: St. Martin's Press, 1996.

Masino, Susan. *The Story of AC/DC: Let There Be Rock*. Madison, Wis.: Omnibus Press, 2006.

Stenning, Paul. *AC/DC: Two Sides to Every Glory: The Complete Biography*. London: Chrome Dreams, 2005.

Walker, Clinton. *Highway to Hell: The Life and Times of AC/DC Legend Bon Scott*. Portland, Ore.: Verse Chorus Press, 2000.

Web Sites

www.acdcpower.net
ACDC Rising Power

www.acdcrocks.com
AC/DC

www.bonscottconcert.com.au/index.html
The Bon Scott Celebration Concert

www.gibson.com/whatsnew/pressrelease/2001/jan24a.html
The Mighty Angus Young

www.guitarplayer.com/story.asp?storyCode=9193
How to Play Like Malcolm Young

www.rockhall.com
Rock and Roll Hall of Fame

accolade—A sign or expression of high praise.

anti-authoritarian—Against strict rules and authority.

asphyxiated—Suffocated.

bawdy—Humorous, but rude and vulgar.

beat band—A musical group that played a form of pop music that developed in the United Kingdom in the early 1960s and was characterized by simple, guitar-dominated lineups and catchy tunes.

criteria—Agreed-upon standards by which things are judged.

decorum—Dignity or correctness that is socially expected.

diverse—Very different or distinct from each other.

double entendres—Remarks that can be taken more than one way, one of them usually sexually suggestive.

dynamic—Characterized by vigorous activity and producing or undergoing change and development.

homage—A show of respect toward someone.

inducted—Admitted someone into an organization.

maladjusted—Unable to cope with everyday social situations and personal relationships.

platinum—A certification indicating that an album or CD has sold one million copies.

psychedelic—Having to do with attempts to recreate the effects achieved by taking mind-altering drugs.

remastered—Improved the master copy of an earlier audio recording to improve the quality of its reproductions.

savvy—Shrewdness and practical knowledge.

stellar—Exceptionally good.

Ethan Schlesinger lives in upstate New York, where he is a freelance author.

Picture Credits

page

2: UPI Photo Archive
8: Timothy A. Clary/AFP
11: UPI Photo Service
13: UPI Photo Service
14: Albert Productions/Star Photo Archive
17: Albert Productions/Star Photo Archive
18: Feature Image Archive
20: Albert Productions/Star Photo Archive
23: Atlantic Records/NMI
24: Foto Feature Collection
27: Albert Productions/Star Photo Archive

29: Atlantic Records/NMI
30: Star Photo Archive
32: Wilberfore Collection
35: Volkman Walter/Foto Feature Collection
37: Wilberfore Images
38: Wilberfore Images
41: Star Photo Archive
42: New Millennium Images
44: UPI Photo Archive
47: Kerrang!/Foto Feature
49: Kerrang!/Foto Feature
50: UPI Photo Service
53: UPI Photo Service
54: William West/AFP/Getty Images

Front cover: Foto Features Collection